394

D1325919

PREP. LIBRARY

THE STORY OF CHRISTMAS

With words adapted from the Gospels

THE STORY OF CHRISTMAS

Jane Ray

ORCHARD BOOKS

For Ellen

ORCHARD BOOKS
96 Leonard Street, London EC2A 4RH
Orchard Books Australia
14 Mars Road, Lane Cove, NSW 2066

First published in Great Britain 1991

© Illustrations by Jane Ray 1991

The right of Jane Ray to be identified as illustrator of this work
has been asserted by her in accordance with the Copyright, Designs
and Patents Act, 1988.
A CIP catalogue record for this book is available from
the British Library.
1 85213 280 9
Printed in Singapore.

In the days of Herod the King, in the town of Nazareth, there lived a young girl named Mary. She was betrothed to a carpenter, whose name was Joseph.

Now the angel Gabriel was sent from God to Nazareth,
to the house where Mary lived. And the angel said,
"Hail, Mary! Blessed are you among women,
for God has chosen you to be the mother of his Son.

You shall give birth to a baby boy, and he shall be called Jesus."

And Mary said, "Let what you have said be done." And the angel left her.

Now it came to pass that while Mary was waiting
for the child to be born, an order went out for every

person to return to the town of his birth, so that a
count could be made of all the people in the land.

And Joseph and Mary left Nazareth together to go

to Bethlehem, where Joseph was born.

When they reached Bethlehem, Mary knew it was
time for the baby to be born. But the town was filled

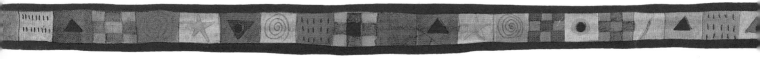

with people and there was no room for them at the
inn. So the innkeeper led them to his stable.

And there Mary gave birth to her son,
and wrapped him in swaddling clothes.
She laid him in a manger,
with the ox and the ass standing by.

Now there were some shepherds in the fields nearby, keeping watch over their flocks by night. And the angel of the Lord appeared before them, and the glory of the Lord shone around.

The shepherds crouched, trembling, among their

sheep but the angel said to them: "Fear not, for I
bring you tidings of great joy! For today in Bethlehem
a child is born and he is Christ the Lord. This is a sign
to you, that you will find the baby wrapped in
swaddling clothes, lying in a manger."

And a great multitude of heaven's angels appeared,
praising God and singing,

"Glory to God in the highest and peace on earth,
goodwill to all men."

The shepherds left their flocks and hurried to the stable; and when they found Mary and Joseph and

the baby lying in the manger, they knelt before him
and worshipped him.

Then they returned home, praising God
for all that they had seen, and all the people

who heard them hastened to Bethlehem
to see the holy baby for themselves.

There came also three wise men from the east, who had seen a bright star in the skies. Bearing gifts, they travelled far across seas and mountains, until they reached the city of Jerusalem.

"Where is the baby who is born to be King?" they asked. "We have seen his star in the east, and have come to worship him."

Now King Herod was troubled when he heard of this
other king, more powerful than himself. And he sent
for the wise men, saying, "Go and search for the child

and return to me once you have found him, so that I
too may come and worship him."
But the King meant to do him harm.

And the star shone bright in the skies,
guiding the wise men onwards,

till it led them to Bethlehem,
and the stable where the baby lay.

And when they found the baby with Mary, his mother, the wise men laid their gifts before him and worshipped him on bended knee.

Then they opened up their treasures for the baby – gold, and frankincense, and myrrh.

But being warned by God in a dream not to return to King Herod, they departed to their own country by another way.

And in time Joseph took Mary and the baby Jesus
home to Nazareth, and the baby grew tall and strong:
and the grace of God was upon him.